IT'S TIME TO LEARN ABOUT BLUE CRANES

It's Time to Learn about Blue Cranes

Walter the Educator

Silent King Books
A WhichHead Entertainment Imprint

Copyright © 2025 by Walter the Educator

All rights reserved. No part of this book may be reproduced in any manner whatsoever without written per- mission except in the case of brief quotations embodied in critical articles and reviews.

First Printing, 2024

Disclaimer

This book is a literary work; the story is not about specific persons, locations, situations, and/or circumstances unless mentioned in a historical context. Any resemblance to real persons, locations, situations, and/or circumstances is coincidental. This book is for entertainment and informational purposes only. The author and publisher offer this information without warranties expressed or implied. No matter the grounds, neither the author nor the publisher will be accountable for any losses, injuries, or other damages caused by the reader's use of this book. The use of this book acknowledges an understanding and acceptance of this disclaimer.

It's Time to Learn about Blue Cranes is a collectible early learning book by Walter the Educator suitable for all ages belonging to Walter the Educator's Time to Eat Book Series. Collect more books at WaltertheEducator.com

USE THE EXTRA SPACE TO TAKE NOTES AND DOCUMENT YOUR MEMORIES

BLUE CRANES

Out in the fields so wide and free,

It's Time to Learn about
Blue Cranes

A tall blue crane walks gracefully.

With feathers soft, so pale and bright,

It shines beneath the morning light.

Its legs are long, so thin and neat,

They help it wade through ponds and creeks.

Step by step, it moves with care,

Looking for food here and there.

Its beak is sharp, its eyes are keen,

It spots a fish in waters clean.

With one quick strike, it grabs a treat,

A tasty snack that's fresh and sweet!

The blue crane loves the open land,

Where grassy fields and rivers stand.

It spreads its wings, so wide, so strong,

And flaps them slowly all day long.

It's Time to Learn about
Blue Cranes

With gentle calls, it sings a tune,

A lovely sound beneath the moon.

It chats with friends both far and near,

So other cranes can always hear.

When it's time to build a nest,

It picks a place that feels the best.

With sticks and grass, so soft and high,

A cozy home beneath the sky.

The mother lays her eggs with care,

The father stays to guard them there.

They wait and watch until one day,

The baby cranes peck out to play!

The little chicks are fluffy and small,

They run and jump but sometimes fall.

Their parents teach them how to stand,

It's Time to Learn about
Blue Cranes

To flap, to stretch, to walk the land.

And soon they grow so tall and grand,

With wings that help them leave the sand.

They learn to fly, so smooth, so high,

And dance like raindrops in the sky.

So if you see a crane one day,

Just watch it dance and wade and play.

A bird so rare, so proud, so true,

It's Time to Learn about
Blue Cranes

The Blue Crane shines in skies so blue!

ABOUT THE CREATOR

Walter the Educator is one of the pseudonyms for Walter Anderson. Formally educated in Chemistry, Business, and Education, he is an educator, an author, a diverse entrepreneur, and he is the son of a disabled war veteran. "Walter the Educator" shares his time between educating and creating. He holds interests and owns several creative projects that entertain, enlighten, enhance, and educate, hoping to inspire and motivate you. Follow, find new works, and stay up to date with Walter the Educator™

at WaltertheEducator.com

www.ingramcontent.com/pod-product-compliance
Lightning Source LLC
LaVergne TN
LVHW052017060526
838201LV00059B/4074